TORPID WIT

THE STAGE OF STUPOR

SUMEET KUMAR

ISBN 979-888546525-0

Sumeet Kumar

Sumeet Kumar , A adult who experiences many phases of love in his life , get broked many times , stands up every time and keep moving to the next phases of the life.In reality he is a writter as well as singer (as a hobby).

Very exciting and interesting fact about him is that he is aauthor of New era i.e. he starts his journey of writing at the age when he was going to schools to get the study . His some famous works i.e. Maturity Of Love (Genre - Love),Privacy For Dream (Genre - Middle Class), Army Squad ofLove (Genre- The Seperation of Army Love), 5 Days of Love(Genre- Temporarily Love), Th e Endearment Of Love(Genre - Historical Era Of Love), Social Destruction Indo-Pak (Genre - The Story of The Love At The Time Of Division Of India And Pakistan), Middle Class Soul (Genre - The Dreams of Middle Class), The Accursed Kanatpur (Genre -The Horrific Story Of A Village), Wrong Number (Genre -The Suspenseful Physco Killer Story), The Secrecy OfDeadly Midnight (Genre - The Suspense About a Crime),Fragile Religious Of Death (Genre- The Death Of A TrustfulPerson), Nature Vs Science (Genre - The Future Battle Between Nature And Science In A Horrific Way), Generic Man (Genre - The Dream of I.I.T), The Unconsious 12 Hours(Genre - The Illusion At Stage Of Comma), The StrangeBurden (Genre - The Burden Of Love) , Her Existence (Genre- The Female Pain In The Society) , Jockstrap Prize (Genre -The True Story Of A National Athlete) , H Man [Hindi] (Genre - Superhero Tragic Story), H Man [English] (Genre - Superhero Tragic Story) , Maturity Of Love [Englsih] (Genre - Love) and many more are available on various geners on the offcial platform of

Amazon, Flipkart and Notionpress. You can buy them
from there.

Contents

Preface

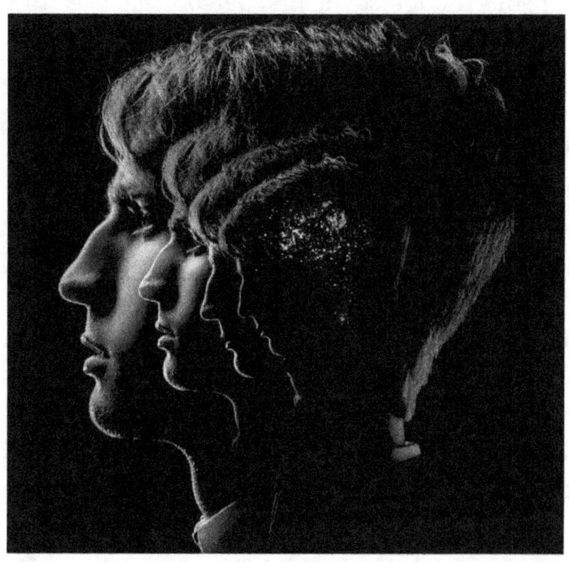

Day dreaming is the edging of consciousness under dates from the current situation tasks when attention drifts to more personal and internal direction. In undefined stages its look like not so much complicated there also undefined stages under show danger complication which beway sometimes beyond the nature rule. Yes they can so side about the day dreaming is a type of undefined external feeling which they can as imagination.this Phenomenon is command in people party life should be a large scale study in which participants spend the real of their walking time on average on day dreaming.the are various types of names including in the fact to describe about the day dreaming sometimes its not behaving like There let it be focused on the names in the fact to describe a daydreaming. Mind wonders spontaneous thoughts. The first person who used the term of dying was Jerome (me) . Singer (February 14/6 /2019) who research programs led the foundation for almost all the most recent research programs led the foundation for almost all the subcent research in this area today. undefined the Yale School of Medicine. He was a fellow of the American Psychological Association the American Association for the Advancement of Science and the New York Academy of Sciences. Daydreaming is also characteristic of people with Attention Deficit Hyperactive Disorder and can be seen in the negative light with us. Tend to have a more difficult time concentrating on their surrodings and begin midfull of current tasks. Actually the way of emotions can also define the fact of day drumming by the help negative and postive vibes. So many differencethinking to define them with a single term .about the negative dreaming it can be defined as a negative mood of others which is a type of another association of dreaming. research funds people generally report a lower happiness rating when the are daydreaming than when they are usually not. The are more likely to be day dream but the finding remains true across all activities.Thefinding remains true across all activities.the important interrelationship between mood and day dreaming fronttime-sound analysis is under the later case first not around the other. Forgetting the way of progress is also a type of fearing behavior that comes under the situation of negative weather but according to me it was not because someone forgets her dreams and his strange events what his own way of love the most after something like that Have nothing to do in our own life like employment. Fear under the children daydream for fear that the children may be liked into "neurosis and apopsychosis".

""STILL WAITING FOR SOMEONE TILL AFTER THE DEATH IS A TYPE OF DAY DREAMING.""

One potential reason is the pay of dreaming is easily private and hidden dressed to theme as orbly cost from external goal directed tasks . it is hard to know and record peoples private thoughts such as personal goals and dreams when day dreaming supports the thought is difficult to Discuss.in the case of daydreaming a person comes upon under time when the want to appear because there whole system of thinking was in Imagination world recent studies a simmingly hidden but important benefit of day dreaming argued under them the motion was not dreaming The name of mind was undefined rest position which is not attentively engaged in external tasks. Rather removing this process people indulges them and reflects on fantasy memories. Benefits are the skills of internal reflection developed in daydreaming tokens emotional application of daily life a Explanation: Personal meaning building process.Despite the deleterious effect of daydreaming aptitude tests which most educational institutions on earth emphasis on et al.argued under it is relevant for children to get the internal reflection skills and possesses higher academic achievement under dreaming ability. Are socially and emotional better of also when the external environment demands very high attention from children is reasonable to believe the useful skills underdeveloped. daydreaming can also be used to imagine social situations human beings and are naturally oriented two company to be socially and naturally Daydreaming acts as past socialcurrencies and future outcomes of imagined events and conversion are imagined. According to research and social cognition have strong overlapping similarities when activated portions of the brain are observed the findings indicate under dreaming of the social is unexplained experience. Only because daydreams are often focused on physical representation of social events experiences and people.

""BAD IMPACT OF LIFE BEHAVE AS A GOOD IMPACT OF SMILE .""

This thought true sometimes the impact of past will always remember the future smile why the bad impact of life behave as a good impact of smile.it's not so easy for rapper son which handles the bundle of emotions in one time when it comes undefined the phase Of day dreaming broke all the desires which contain as a realistic stage for under person in a single second.This is likely because day dreams are often focused on the mental representations of social events experiences and people.it was also observed under a large potential Working day dreams approximately 71% were social . According to recent research it was also found that positivityway Romanthan (Deep Thought) could increase in theming of positive future events even in depressed people on the opposite end of spectrum negative negative events. In depressed individuals but did not cause increase in thoughts of negative future events independent individuals but did not cause a significant.

> **"DONT WAIT FOR THE END OF TWLIGHT JUST START THE THE NEW PHASE OF AFFECTION WITH LUMINOSITY"**

> **"If Someone had made a history No one can change the history"**

Acknowledgements

Aman Kumar

Special Thanks to **Aman Kumar** who worked so hard in the preparation of this book. He has continually put with my passive voice, omission of words, and late night calls. You have be en wonderful. Thanks to him for his precious time in reviewing proposals , individual chapters and early drafts, along with his suggestions on the applicability of the material to the world.

I

Stuper

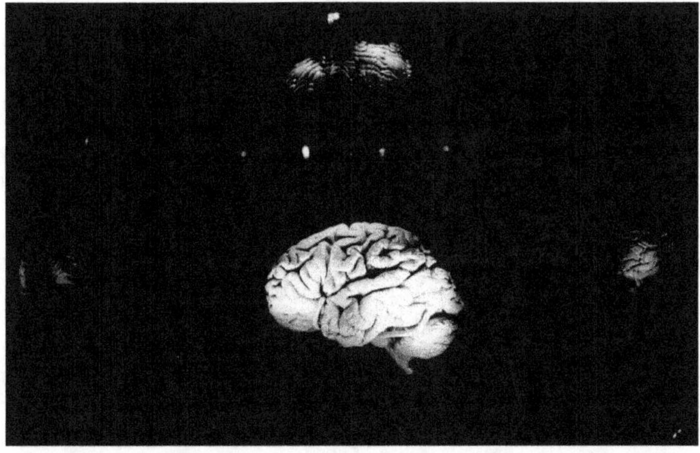

Leaving the existence a mystery, I am also aware of it
that there are some facts which are told by the passing of
time, then they will be judged. That my imagination has
also become aware of the destination of reality somewhere.
If I say straight, I am a coma patient, for only twelve hours,

my life is kind of like that in my pond too, I have to spend twelve hours of courage. I can only do all my work, I can do it in twelve hours, there are no laughing moments in patient life, it is necessary that my whole life is only an accident. Do not see, nor have I ever come to know about the beauty of her waist, because at the time when she is singing, say this, at the time when her custom becomes the face of the face, when my glasses leave me and become someone else's wish. Well my whole life is the same. There is no such accident behind my shin's helplessness. I can tell you all about it, if it is written in silence in my childhood writings, then why only twelve hours of the day, why not the poor, if I had to keep away from the moon's gaze, it would have made me blind anyway. The moonlight of the night, the one who does not see the glow, is the witness of what work I have no problem with mirror loss It is a bit rare and work is also because of the grace of my identity , I tell you to make everyone aware first. By the way, my name identity is also very clear of my helplessness, I mean where I can not see the beauty of the night, nor can I see the light of my waist. that identity was also the same thing, Zain mirza (The God Light is undefined, it is also a fact that I can see my life only for twelve hours, that means I can live it, I can adopt every one of his wishes, I can see myself in its light. I can imagine that, I can feel the force of the wind, I can feel the feet Snow and and in those twelve hours. The doctors say about my helplessness that it is some kind of daydreaming, it is also some kind of coma, it has only one meaning that neither the woman can ever be well aware of my helplessness nor my family members and even I will never know about it. Couldn't compete completely, my life is always imprisoned in the silence of those walls where the sunlight comes Only and only fun is only for twelve hours, my life is very long, man has no compulsion, in reality, when the whole world makes you realize that the pond of something in you is incomplete, then say that the grace of the heart also says it. I have never felt that when I was in the shadow of my mother, I never felt that I was compelled to leave her world and become in someone else's world, only then my feet also started saying that it was not for me. It is said that there is no tradition of breaking it because its gift is an startment. It starts with some pain, and it was only twelve hours in the description of my pain. The writing of my pain was written when I met my love, that too not in reality, but in my story, the point was just so right that I knew about its existence. I was aware of my feet only in my silence. My love was just like my silence. I couldn't conquer my feet because on one side there was helplness that everyone was aware of and on one side the silence that only and only was aware of. By the way, there is no such desperate moment in my life, I have to mention it a long time ago. I had no idea that it would become my life going forward With this is the foot in front of us who is possible Because of my helplessness, I had only one friend, all of them used to call me a ghost, as soon as twelve hours of the day passed, I would say goodbye at the time and after that only a coma patient would remain and nothing else. The feet were probably completely alive, so that the sound of everything would reach his ears, so that the feet would never know after hearing them. made my Existence cultural why does he like this and Why I am different From Others Mayon always used to ask only one question to his mother that mother, when you knew that my life was incomplete, then why did you keep me with yourself, why didn't you separate me from yourself? I say only one blessing for all. I am incomplete, you are the ache of my marriage, my child, you are the reason of my smile , It was already done, the feet were in their eyes, the reason was their reason. Seeing all that, I was hurting myself, I wanted to make my helpleness in any way possible. I only came to know when I asked this question to my mother because everyone had told intelligence that you should drop your child or else you will get troubled later than that, how will you face the mirror society and it will not let you live in the eyes of everyone. Nor did my mother suffer many such miseries even after all this, even when she never left me, whenever the shadow of any trouble fell on me, only and only my mother's love could be seen at the time of the party. Taught me the way of living, not mother kindness, whatever I am today, because of my mother, if my helpness is worse than me, then Because of this, how my feet change my condition, its handwriting is still not fixed, so I will not do any more exhibition and will tell to celebrate my salvation.

"Now I am broken. I have to say this in my eyes.
I do not see in my eyes, I do not see the gift and you say,
I have a lot of love.
It is the one who has kept me alive till today. In my gathering,
there was a saying of the path and also the legend of Mamta.
Everyone has the intention to keep me away from my gathering.
There was a conspiracy to perish."

II
The Way Of Agony

The beginning has also started with a mystery, there is no way, nor any knowledge of the destination, where everyone's pond is pure, leaving me in the captivity of helplessness, no one else can feel it. Entire life would not have passed in the price of money, if I did not get my corn, then my life is incomplete even without twelve hours, I am not able to fulfill my condition. It is incomplete, so without spending time, I take you all into my world, I have got only twelve hours of education in the world to live. 1982 Faridabad city Lucknow I do not have any special memories of my childhood, neither I nor my family ever made it special Mind because he was also somewhere with his feet in his place, after all, who was adopted to an abnormal child, agreed with each and every condition of him, in life everyone has only and only the pond of the Frog, he takes us forward in his destination, if the same care In someone's luck, there is no determination of the Frog, he leaves his destination. Gives me a chance to take her place, my mother never did this Because she never considers us like others, because she is probably her love for us, she is the grace of her love, she is her life, I do not know why my mother made me aware of every single destination of this world when I It was not worth it, he never made me realize that I am weak, I am imprisoned in someone's helplessness all the time, I still remember when the log used to say about me that it is over, it will become dead again and many people They also used to say that now it is time, let's go to the house, otherwise this soul will not let us live, in the fate of childhood, it was never felt that I myself am the reason for a pain. Leaving the (adult)'s ache has become a problem, so even because of the trouble, it started to feel like a curse in childhood. When I was in my mother's mind, I used to forget everything, did not feel anything, only her happiness was visible, whenever I went to her, my dear beta spoke and hugged me, what did I know that I would be able to control her own happiness, the pain is that share . Whose pond once shared a whole lot, rather he used to trouble everyone who is associated with man and I was the only witness, my dad left me because of my mother's only mistake at that time that she chose me in place of her family To the young son who gave him nothing but trouble since childhood, their relationship was broken only on the day when he was born. The feet were undefined for only twelve hours, so the teachings of the society grew to the extent that even toad any relationship in a moment and do not even confess about it, were aware of my truth, so they gave me every reason to live. I have made it difficult, I mean that my brothers and sisters do not like it It was when someone called him a relative of the dead, so he left me because I had made it long ago, it only means that he used to tell me not to keep me with him because if you see the grace of ferocity in your stomach, then you There may be one foot for the whole world, but your pain is one thing. For someone, you leave your relationship at the very first time. I had forced my existence to be the cause of only one pain in his existence, he was nothing else for him. It is said that if the trouble is completely met in a day, then its tradition can also be erased. And the scar of my pain was only for me, and for my family, how could anyone erase that teaching? Good moments don't last forever and bad times never leave. If you see, this heart breaks itself from inside, my helplessness makes me feel sick. And my moms silence was also felt. Dad told mother that we entrust this special orphan house to abnormal human center where neither it will cause any problem and they will take care of it, still my mother said that my zain will stay with me Neither doggy nor will you ever hurt it with yourself and what has happened to you, teenager, this is our own son, understand our feet Fatima, this is not normal, if we grew up with other children, then he himself is always different from them I will feel that you have given birth to it foot it does not mean that I should put my other children's future in danger because of this, it is my son too undefined not teen if it was your son then you would never leave him neither its mother Being a father, I have given birth to you, insisting to send you to Share fan house, I have raised it in my stomach for nine months, I am a beta and I will never get rid of it by myself, I will not be able to live it. We have to leave both of our children, neither can I keep it with me now.I don't even have a pond to become the father of a dead person, if you tell me to keep it with you, you will have to forget us and your two children too. This was the last night when I was close to my mother, was with my family (in life) There are some situations where we do not live wrongly, our feet make us wrong, that too in the eyes of those who do a lot of love. Hua mother never used to tell me to separate from herself, she could live without me even for a moment The duty was to be fulfilled that she could not leave her two children alone nor her husband because what to do, that heart also belonged to an Indian, first of all, for a woman, her family is everything, she was probably not part of them because in me alone I could never have given them the happiness of the whole family, in the same way, I came to know then that my love was probably in my pocket. It was only opponent, I had started getting away from his love, I was starting to suffer a lot from him, it was felt by his existence that all those who left with me were not wrong, it was also realized soon when his love I broke my heart.

**""We need only a pond of darkness, because today
we see light in our eyes (2) of that sun,
yet we had never heard of any infidelity at the
time,
the condition changes, but today only man has
changed in someone's love.... ""**

One day mom and dad dropped me off the orphan house I didn't know the place well because I was engrossed in a few days just a few days the silence was not letting me live Was feeling the right pain I was feeling scared, I was saying this, the loneliness of this world has kept my happiness away from me, this pain was a lot of work, only my family wanted it, only and only my mother's love was needed and nothing else. Feet without help, time took me that too China, it was happening in four walls, feet were being broken only and only for twelve hours, say that the gathering which I had left, the gathering had now become the reason for my existence, the helplessness in my home I was facing the helplessness coming to the house, even my helplessness did not hurt me that identity was helpless and home too.

""We have come to a strange gathering, where no one is our own,
nor any other foreigner we have seen the pond of life,
I have seen the glasses where twilight is saying about glimpse of beauty.""

It is still possible to write a donation for one thing, mother used to belong with a Muslim family, my father was from a Hindu family, it clearly means that both belonged to a different religion, the heart wanted something like this, their love made the tradition of religion. He wiped out the next story, neither mother has told me nor did I wish to ask him. Time is a little graceful, so now you have to wait for the moment, you all have to say to go to my full story

"

"My pain

shows a manship
my thoughts too
narrated the identity of mine"”

III
The Consciousness

The silence, which was capable of suffering, was making me feel an escape every time. In such a way that the fanna started showing some kind of revenge, I took that step, which no one was aware of, was aware of the level of my pain, I am also telling what silence in the public's tiredness to pinhan inside myself, despite knowing everything, I Let it happen that the love of the family was never lucky, thinking that the education was of two types, first we feel our pain like a patient, on the other hand, by feeling it in happiness. Alvi says to the soul , my clap was the second time, I had murdered the pond of my life, I tried to kill myself at the time when everyone was sleeping secretly, the chase broke, I was aware of my condition, whatever made me tired Do not do it before twlight, that means after seeing the rituals of those twelve hours. (The desire of the heart and mind is also strange. The thought that we have a pond, then these two are with us, thinking that it is incomplete to complete the pond. Then he is far from me , will I be able to get my monthly now again, I will be able to tell them that there is a conspiracy in the body of leaving you all, more than the tradition of twelve hours in the name of leaving me, the reality of all of you leaving me from them It hurts me more than my childhood Is making me aware of the silliness of the path. The tale of time made both of them suffer, at the time when he was trying to kill himself, even at the same time he jumped in a river. Some of the people of Orphan saw me, went after me to catch me, he started running from him, while running away, he went to some place which was far from the Orphan house. It is about to happen that the legend I had separated from myself was going to be difficult for me for some time, that means I tried to die again but someone's grace stopped me. The tradition of seeing the spectacles was gone, that means when the twelve hours were over, I did not know when I was running away from it, so my watch which used to warn me when the twelve hours were over, I may have fallen somewhere while running. Looking at the good times, I had forgotten his identity, for the first time when I closed my eyes, I felt that I was going to get a new life, even though I had fainted at the time, I could hear everything. That voice was the reason everyone was feeling there was only one thing that I was not aware of at the time, from his face.

> **"Weird helplessness
> because nor this Me
> saying of the way gives
> is and is not only me live Of
> narrated."**

The silence after which I had spent many years, now she was going to be worse than me, only after meeting her feet, I was helplessly going away from me. Those who were the identity of the first prison , they were the reason for my happiness, also only because of one word, remember when he took me rock one by one. He was in love with her, made that happiness in my eyes, his words made me want to take the path away from myself. Why is it gonna happen? This was the time of which I was unaware, after all this, when I woke up the next day, my wish was looking for a glimpse of her, after all, who is she? No, I don't see any dreams, I'm going to give my life Saw no one found the foot, found that beautiful voice, because of which I had just erased the pond of the path, started looking for it, the joint started peeling from the joint that there is someone? Still no one answered, it was already felt enough Another complication of my illness was that I go to sleep after twelve hours, after waking up, I feel a lot of pain, I could not even do that for a while, I could not think of anything for the rest of the day, I was unconscious all day. Seeing all this, I waited for a while, I saw that some logs are coming, I felt that the voice due to which I have been trained to live again, maybe it should also be included in them, when I went outside and saw it, it was not there either. (You all must be thinking that how

I came to know that he is not him, so how did I know that he was never able to meet him). Because when I What I told him about the baatis was the conversation who knew about me, when i asked about him, he said that we only saved you from jumping into the lamp, you had fainted, saved your life, about which you are mentioning. You are doing no such girl has come, about whom are you asking if no one comes in the dense forest, so our ancestors used to live there for many years and now we. (What was this mean? What was it, was it not the reality, my she was sitting on the back of my imagination, say juth is not speaking to me, why would he speak lie to me? I don't even know this story very well from me Somewhere the answer was that we have saved you the net, we have brought you this. That day my silence had doubled because I felt that my whole life was now a lonely foot. I still did not trust those people, why not this foot My heart was not ready that his words were just my dream, it is just a dream, I asked him again a question that for how many days I was unconscious then he said that you were unconscious for the whole four days undefined feet how can this be ever Adultery cannot remain unconscious for a day, nor was there any such accident that day, which gives me four days of being unconscious, then I started to feel that why this lie infront of me .

"I will not tell you to come back.
They were some of the friends who are still
there somewhere,
you can make them away from me, otherwise
whatever is the habit of living,
will also be lost somewhere."

Bash only one question, my whole life was lost, why and how was she who taught the love of living how to live: she didn't teach the accident was the right time, the feet had become a pond of her words. The narration of power had increased, wanted to erase his helplessness for the sake of his love, maybe the time of training was long enough to meet him, perhaps. It has not even started yet and you are talking about ending your intention. I don't want to complete it. Even though my story is incomplete, my feet like wish are not my hope. My love had become helpless for me at the same time, even a question, why did he do this? Do those logs really don't know Even knowing that they were giving some deception to me, the tradition of understanding the time had become so difficult for me that I could not understand anything, what should I do John I can never go to my house It had become a suffocation for me, even then there was a desire to live because I wanted to be able to compete with him, I told him whether I would like to live for a few days. I can't even think of it, for this he was saying even before I said, you stop now because your condition is not good now, after waiting for four months, when did not know anything, which helplessness I was in love with him in his past, but only in his love, waiting in love just teaches the story of the path She teaches me to stay alive till then. Waiting for her, when will I meet her in my only one room?

"Take your path along with you, know you are a
traveller,
then keep on moving towards your
destination.
Many people have come to stop you again."